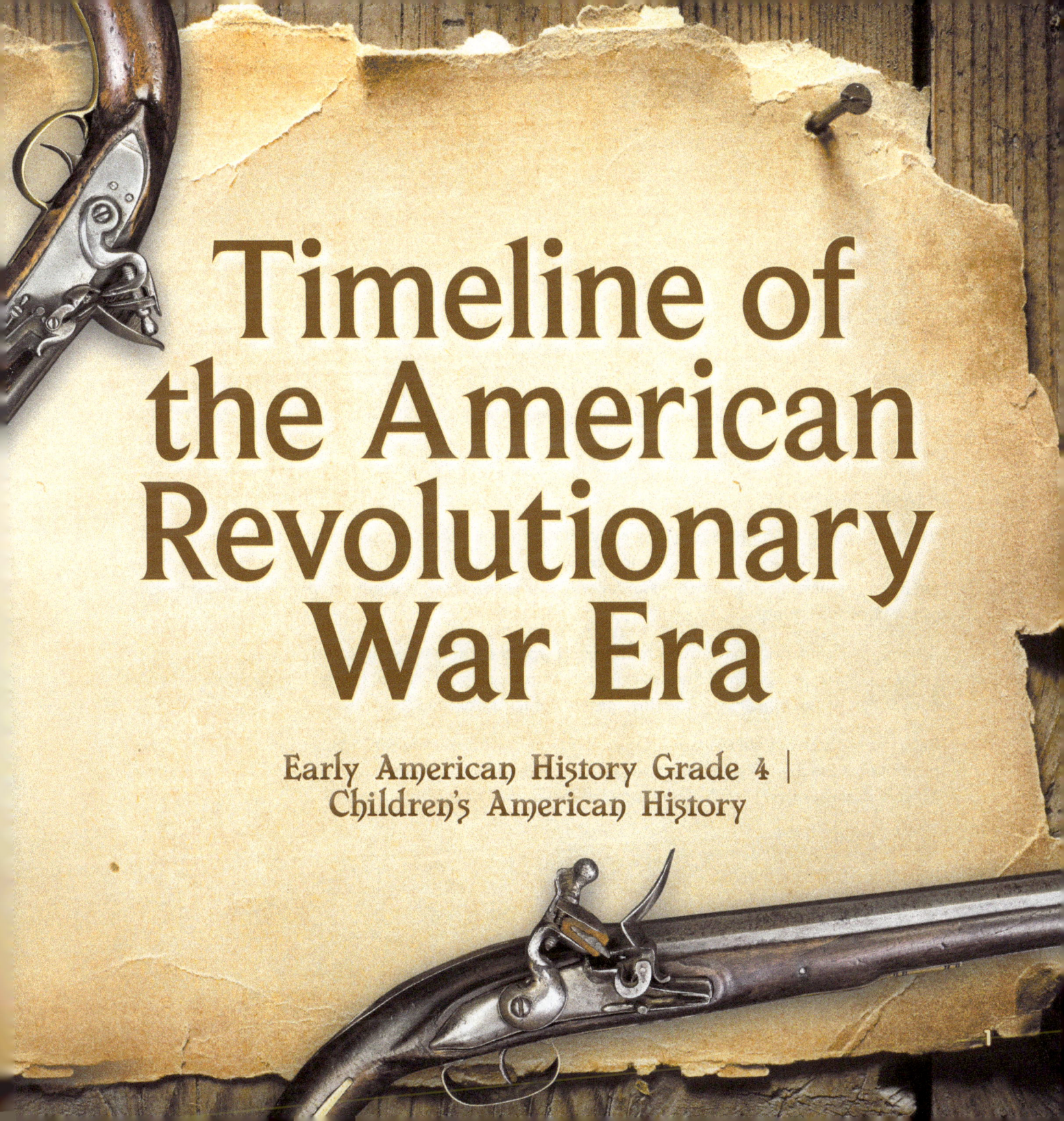

Timeline of the American Revolutionary War Era

Early American History Grade 4 |
Children's American History

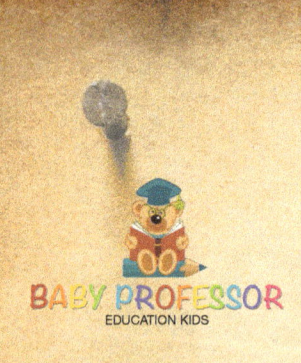

BABY PROFESSOR
EDUCATION KIDS

First Edition, 2020

Published in the United States by Speedy Publishing LLC, 40 E Main Street, Newark, Delaware 19711 USA.

© 2020 Baby Professor Books, an imprint of Speedy Publishing LLC

Baby Professor Books are available at special discounts when purchased in bulk for industrial and sales-promotional use. For details contact our Special Sales Team at Speedy Publishing LLC, 40 E Main Street, Newark, Delaware 19711 USA. Telephone (888) 248-4521 Fax: (210) 519-4043.

10 9 8 7 6 * 5 4 3 2 1

Print Edition: 9781541959781
Digital Edition: 9781541962781

See the world in pictures. Build your knowledge in style.
www.speedypublishing.com

Table of Contents

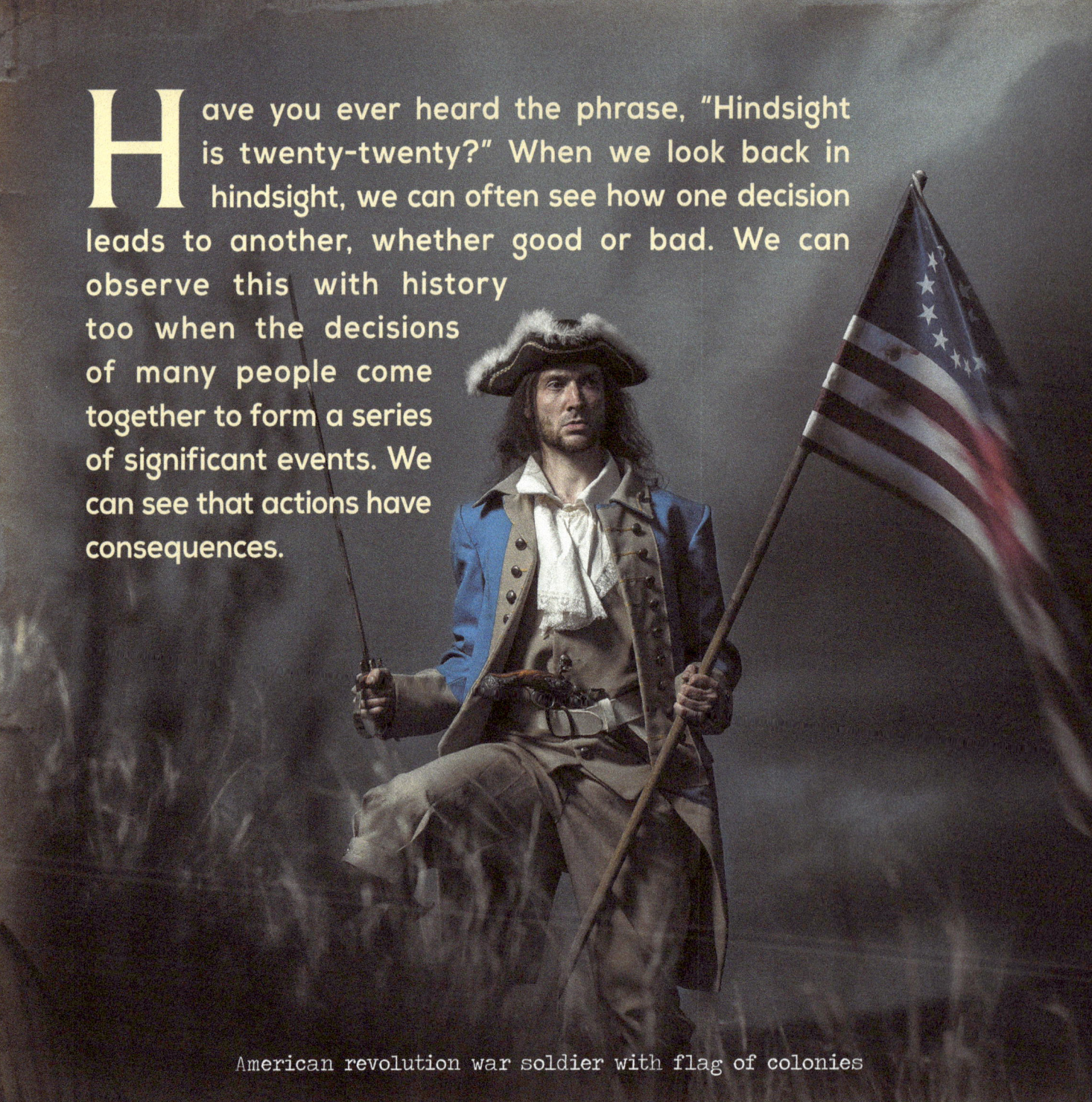

Have you ever heard the phrase, "Hindsight is twenty-twenty?" When we look back in hindsight, we can often see how one decision leads to another, whether good or bad. We can observe this with history too when the decisions of many people come together to form a series of significant events. We can see that actions have consequences.

American revolution war soldier with flag of colonies

There were many things that happened during the American Revolutionary War era which ultimately resulted in the establishment of the United States of America. This book will discuss the timeline of the American Revolutionary War from 1775 to 1783. It was this war that allowed the thirteen British colonies in North America to separate and become the United States of America.

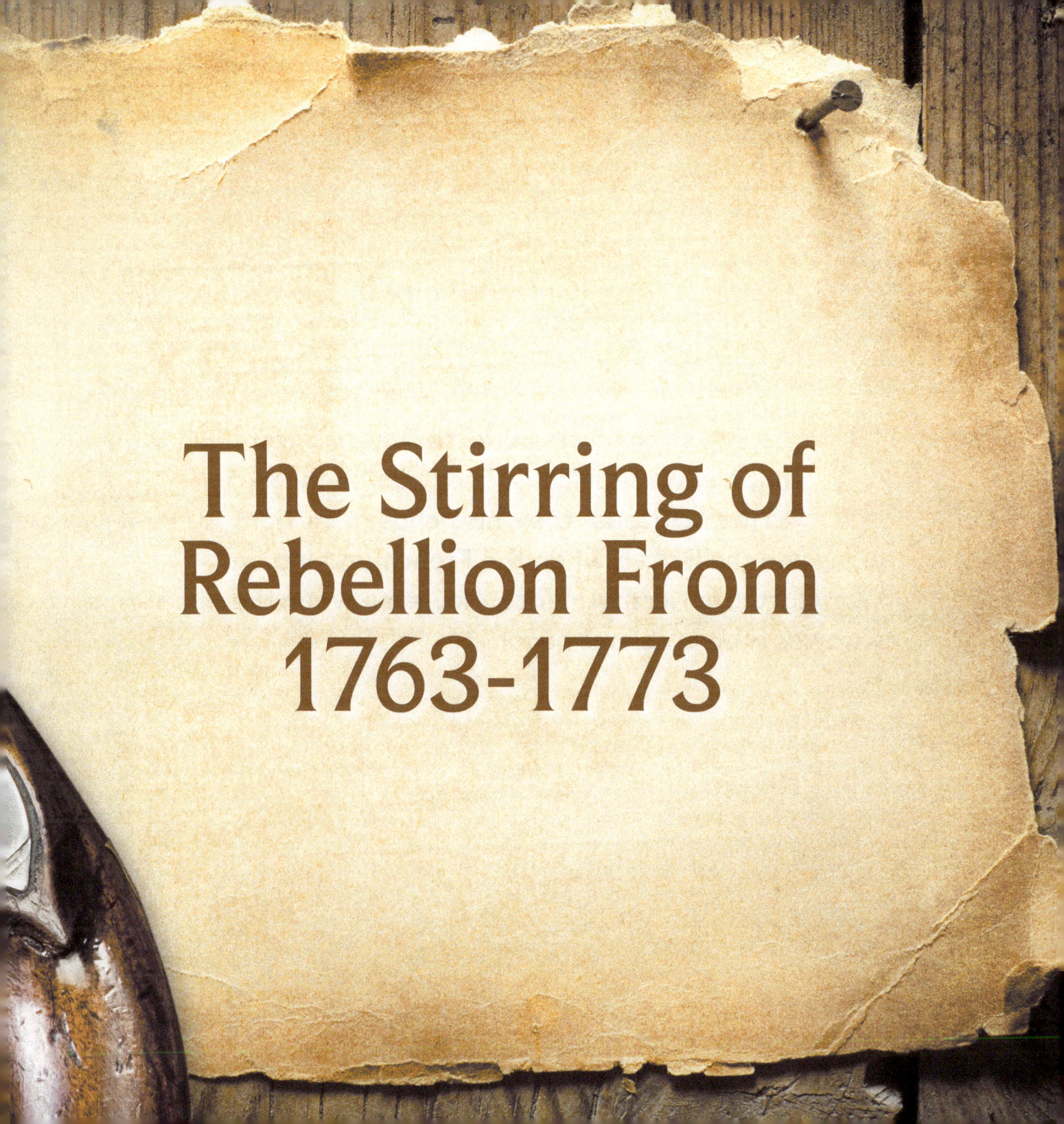

The British colonists in North America were not always rebellious. They had been loyal British citizens; they had chosen to fight alongside the British when the French and Indian War started in North America. However, when the war was over, problems began.

British soldiers marching through wilderness to Fort Duquesne, Pennsylvania during the French and Indian War, 1755.

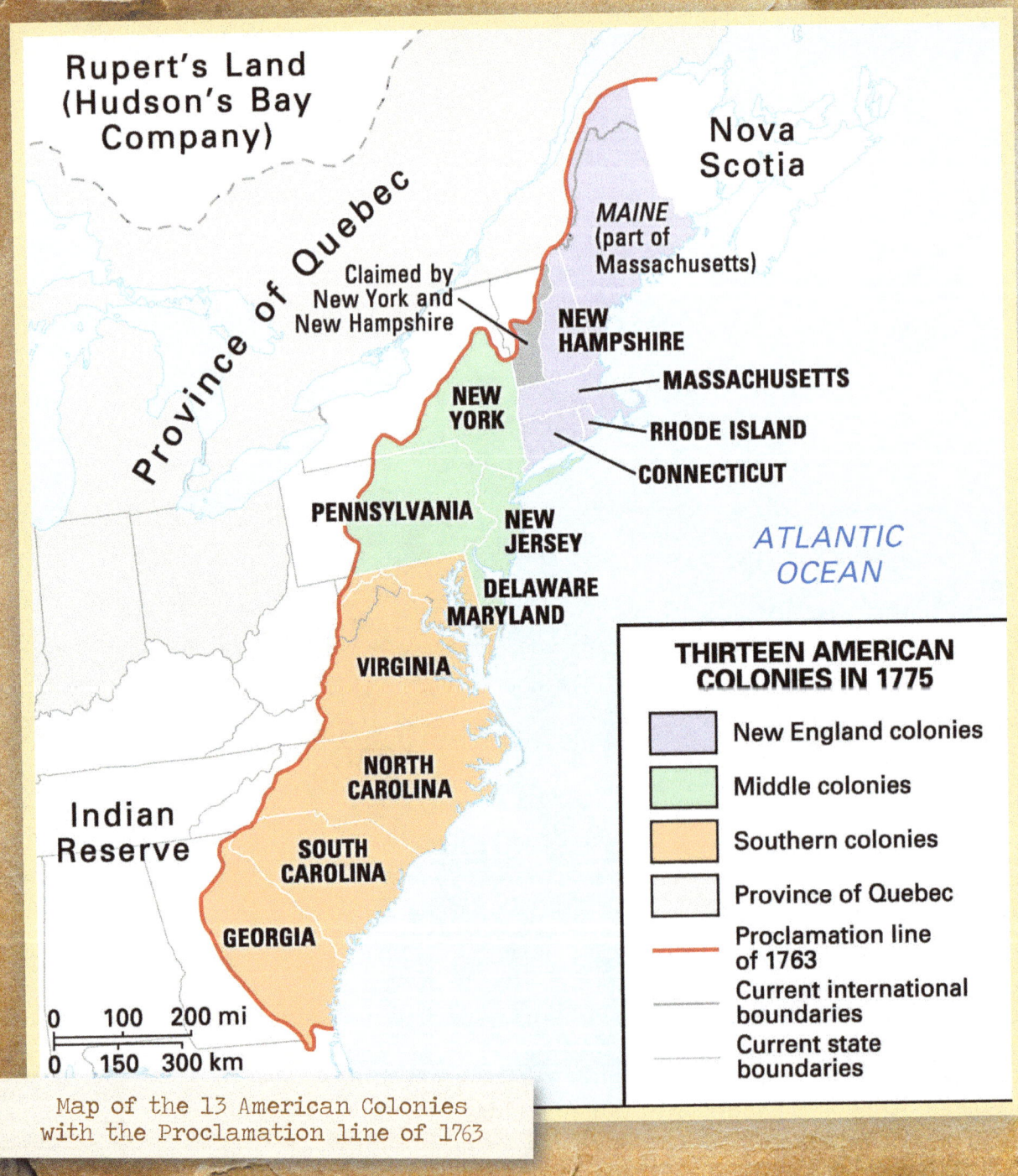

Map of the 13 American Colonies
with the Proclamation line of 1763

The colonists were alarmed when the king, with the Royal Proclamation of 1763, forbid them from going to farm in areas of land to which they felt they had earned the right. They had fought in the French and Indian War, in part to gain more land. Now they could not even settle in the land they had won. Some people, like George Washington, had even been promised land there.

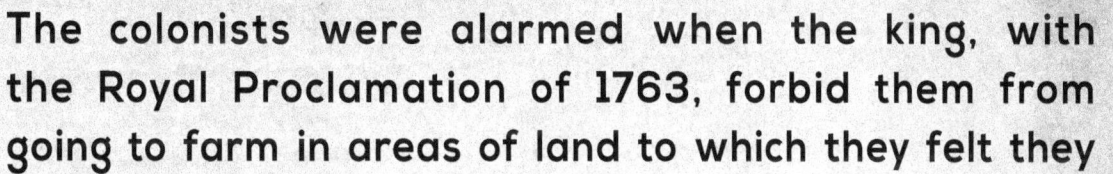

The Royal Proclamation of 1763

The British king was worried about agitating the Native Americans, but that was not a major concern for the colonists. It seemed wrong that a king who lived in Britain, so far away from the American colonies, should interfere so much in the colonists' lives. The colonists also noticed that although many of their men had fought and died alongside the men from England, they were paid less. This seemed grievously unfair.

King George III

British troops entering Boston to enforce taxation and other colonial legislation before the American Revolution.

Regardless, the French and Indian War had cost Britain a lot of money. The British government now intended to focus more on its colonies to gain a profit for their efforts. Also, the colonists were expected to provide the money to pay for the soldiers sent to keep the land and protect them from retaliation after the war. The British government implemented the Sugar Act in 1764 to gain more taxes.

Then it implemented the Quartering Act forcing the colonists to take in any British soldier that demanded it. It did not, however, require the soldiers to be polite or decent. They could easily take advantage of the colonists.

British soldiers quartered in an
American colonial home, 1770s.

Colonists demanding the
withdrawal of the British Army.

The colonists became increasingly angry with the British government. They did not want soldiers to protect them. They had proven in the war that they could protect themselves. Why would they pay for soldiers and be forced to shelter them when they could take care of themselves? Why did they have to pay unfair taxes when no one represented them in the British government? How was that fair?

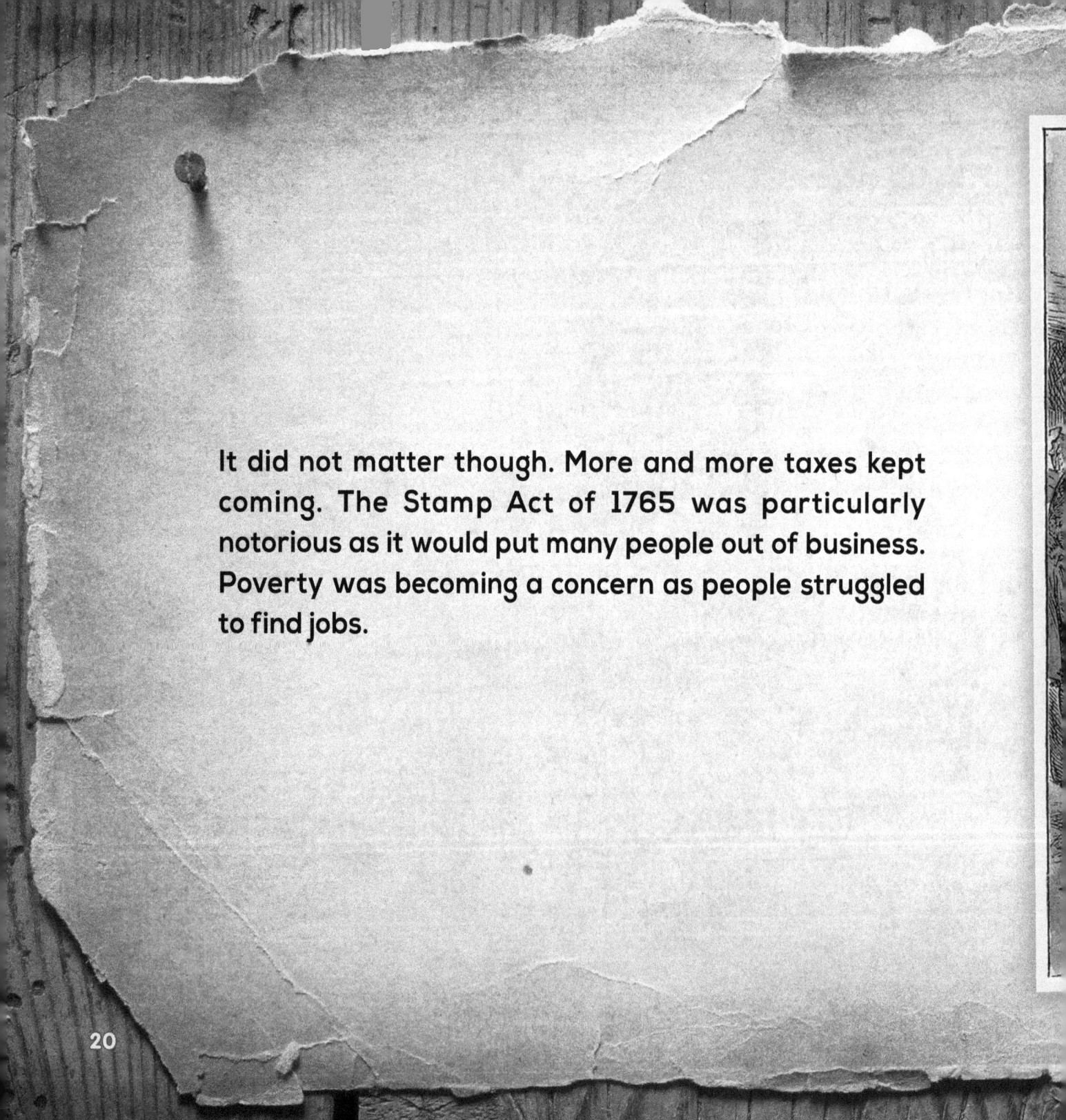

It did not matter though. More and more taxes kept coming. The Stamp Act of 1765 was particularly notorious as it would put many people out of business. Poverty was becoming a concern as people struggled to find jobs.

Bostonians reading news of the Stamp Act in August, 1765.

Samuel Adams

In response, a group called the Sons of Liberty was created. It was started by Samuel Adams but spread around the colonies to fight against the injustice.

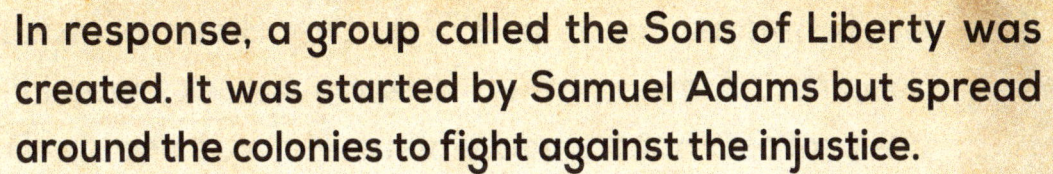

Sons of Liberty marching with an effigy of a stamp master to protest the Stamp Act in Boston, 1765

As tensions rose, in 1770, the Boston Massacre occurred. A man named Crispus Attucks was killed in the protest that turned violent. He was shot by British soldiers. He is often considered the first person to have been killed for American freedom.

The Boston Massacre, 5 March 1770, with Crispus Attucks shown prominently in the center foreground.

Crispus Attucks

Boston Tea Party, December 16, 1773

Finally, when the notorious Tea Act was passed, the tide of fury could not be stopped. Revolutionaries boarded British trade ships and dumped overboard all their tea that they had intended to trade. The British responded with harsh laws and harsher taxes, which the locals called the Intolerable Acts. Boston ports were closed until the colonists paid back the price of the lost tea and martial law was established in Massachusetts. Stifled and threatened under the might of the British military, the colonists realized that the only way to gain their freedom was to fight.

The War Begins

In 1774, when the King ignored the colonists' plea to remove the Intolerable Acts, the colonists began to prepare for battle. Men from all walks of life began to work together to train. They called themselves "minutemen" as they might have to be ready at a "minute's notice."

Minutemen of the American Revolution

The British decided to stop this rebellion in its infancy. In 1775, they went to Concord to seize weaponry and supplies stored by the colonists, who now called themselves the patriots. They would fail.

Minutemen fight to hold off the British army at Concord Bridge, April 10, 1775.

Paul Revere would famously ride through the countryside to warn the minutemen.

Paul Revere warns that the British are coming, 1775.

Two battles were fought at Lexington and Concord. On April 19, 1775, the Revolutionary War began.

The Battles of Lexington and Concord were the first military engagements of the American Revolutionary War.

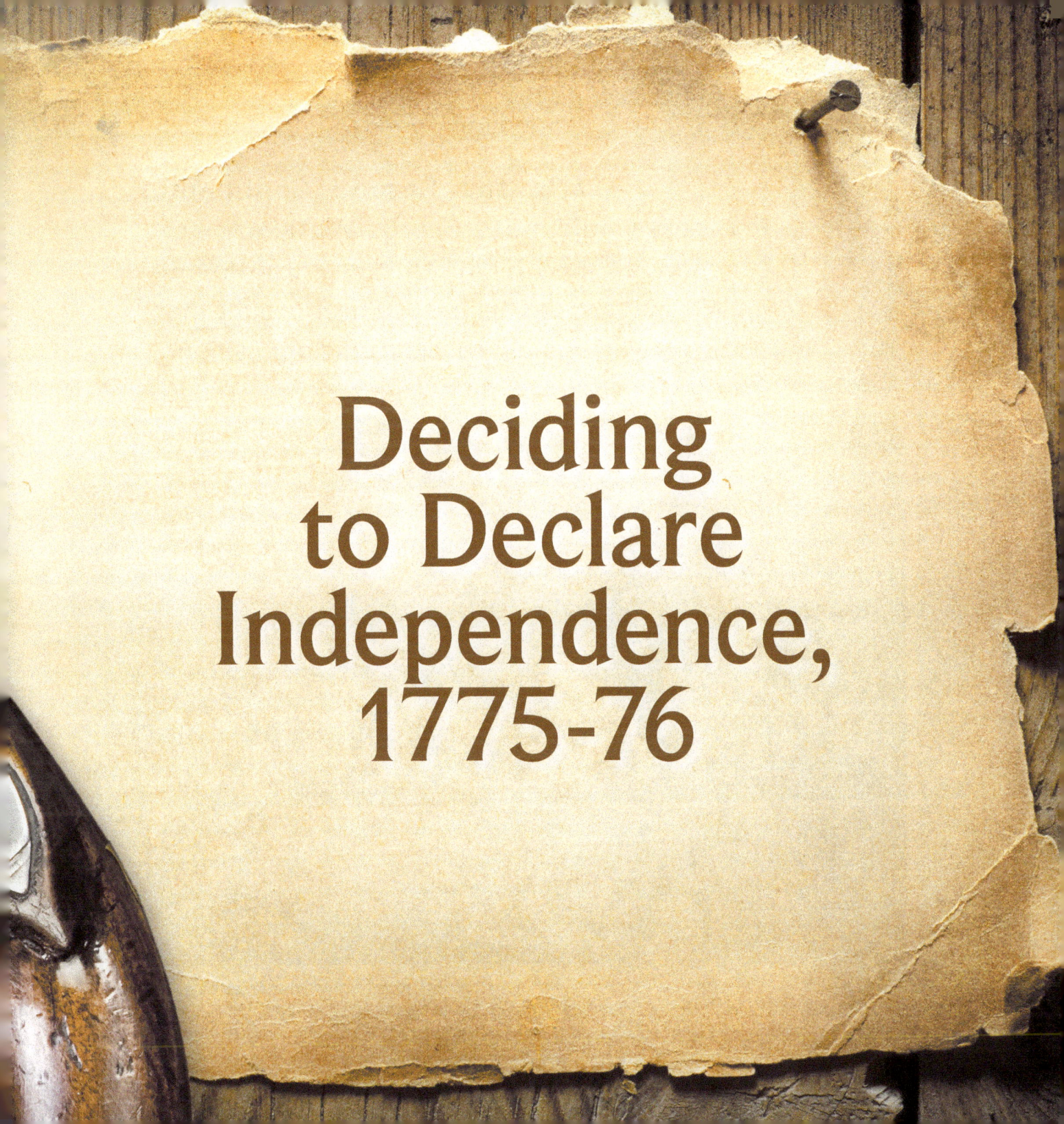

In May of 1775, the Second Continental Congress would make George Washington the commander-in-chief of the new Continental Army. Washington did his best to prepare his men, but they were up against considerable opposition.

George Washington taking command of the Continental Army at Cambridge, Massachusetts, July 3, 1775.

The British had a powerful military and their navy was considered the best at the time. However, the patriots were determined. While they lost the first major battle of the war in Bunker Hill, which was not far from Boston, the Continental Army killed so many British soldiers that the patriots held out hope.

Battle of Bunker Hill

It would not be easy. Even though the men had believed the war would be over quickly. Washington even assured his wife that he would be home by Christmas; the war would drag on. In 1775 many colonists had hoped to make the king see how serious they were and then come to a compromise with them. By 1776, it was resoundingly clear, however, that separation was the only option. On July 4th of that year, the Declaration of Independence would be approved. The thirteen colonies would become the United States of America.

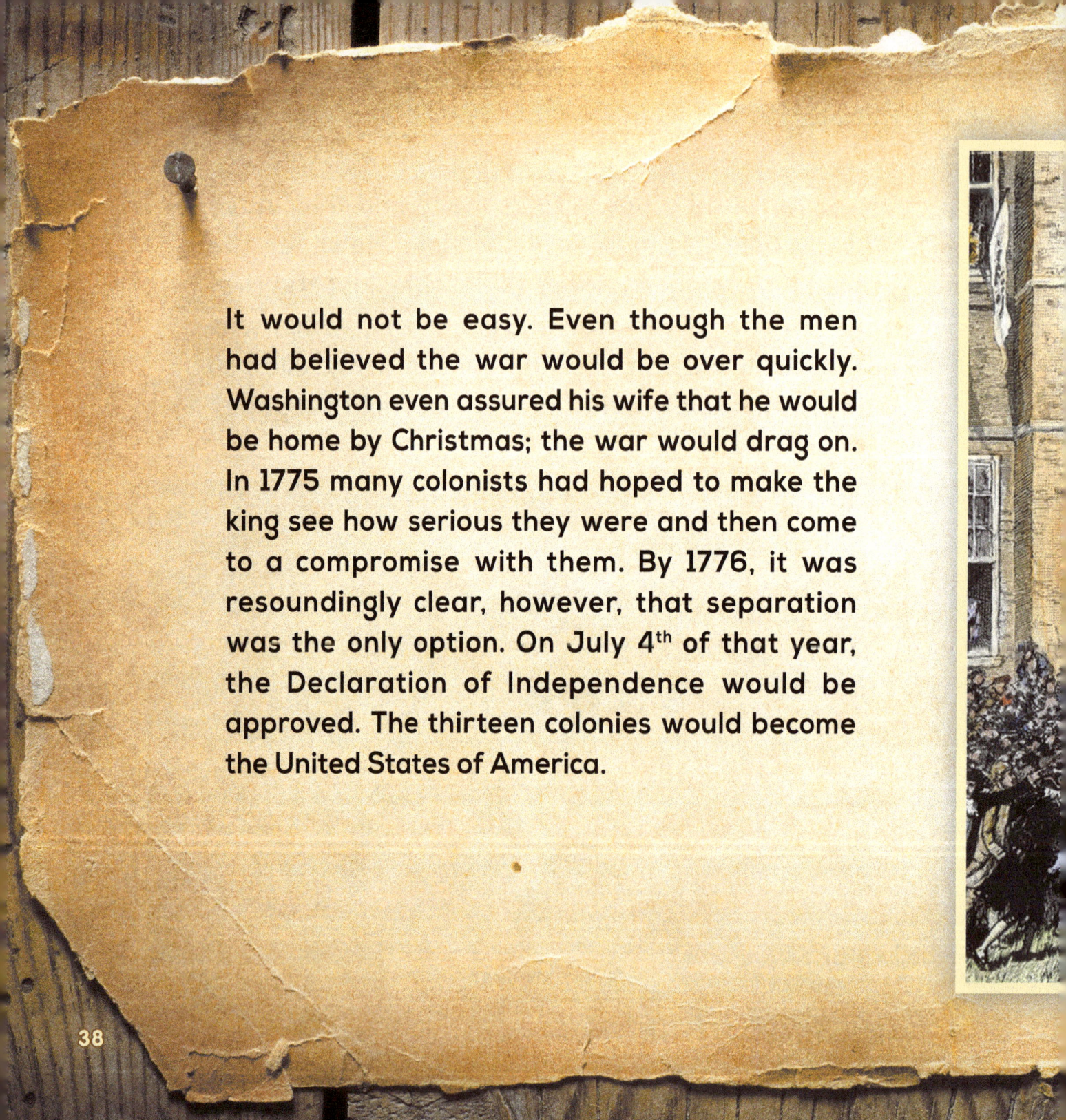

Reading the Declaration of Independence to cheering colonists in Philadelphia, July 4, 1776.

George Washington reads the Declaration of Independence to the Continental Army. July 9, 1776.

George Washington read this new document aloud to his soldiers to motivate them. Now that it was clear the war would be lasting longer, it was critical to keep morale up. Most of the men who had joined the army had expected to be home by 1776. With the war lasting so long, there was not enough food, equipment, or clothing for the soldiers. If they did not believe in what they were fighting for enough to persevere, the war would be lost very quickly.

Battle Tactics in the North, 1776-77

The British drove the outclassed Continental Army out of New York. The Americans would be driven back all the way to Pennsylvania. They were simply outnumbered and out-supplied. However, George Washington was cunning. He had fought with the British in the French and Indian War and knew where their weaknesses were. His army knew the land better and if they could surprise the British, they could win.

Retreat of the Continental army from Long Island after defeat by the British, 1776.

Taking advantage of the British soldiers enjoying Christmas celebrations, Washington stealthily crossed the Delaware River back into New Jersey where he would lead his men to some important battles.

George Washington crossing the Delaware River during the Battle of Trenton in December 1776.

George Washington leading the Americans at the Battle of Princeton, New Jersey.

The victories that they had in Trenton and Princeton would serve to keep hope alive. While it was true that they were not able to face the British might head on, it was clear that with the right strategy, there was a chance.

General Horatio Gates

This principle held true in the next year in October of 1777 when General Horatio Gates would lead the Americans to victory in the Battle of Saratoga. This was a very important battle, because it drew the attention of the French. The French had lost their last war with the British and decided they would support the Americans in their fight for independence. This not only gave the Continental Army some much needed support in supplies, but also experienced officers willing to help train the men.

The surrender of British Lt General John Burgoyne to American General Horatio Gates after the Battle of Saratoga in 1777.

Winter at Valley Forge, 1777-78

No significant battles happened during the winter that the Continental Army spent in Valley Forge. It was customary for armies at that time to not engage in battle due to the difficult weather. Washington decided to use that time to get his men some much needed training. The British were wasting away their winter in Philadelphia which they had captured earlier in the year.

George Washington leading the Continental
Army to Valley Forge winter camp.

George Washington in the Continental Army's camp in Valley Forge, Pennsylvania.

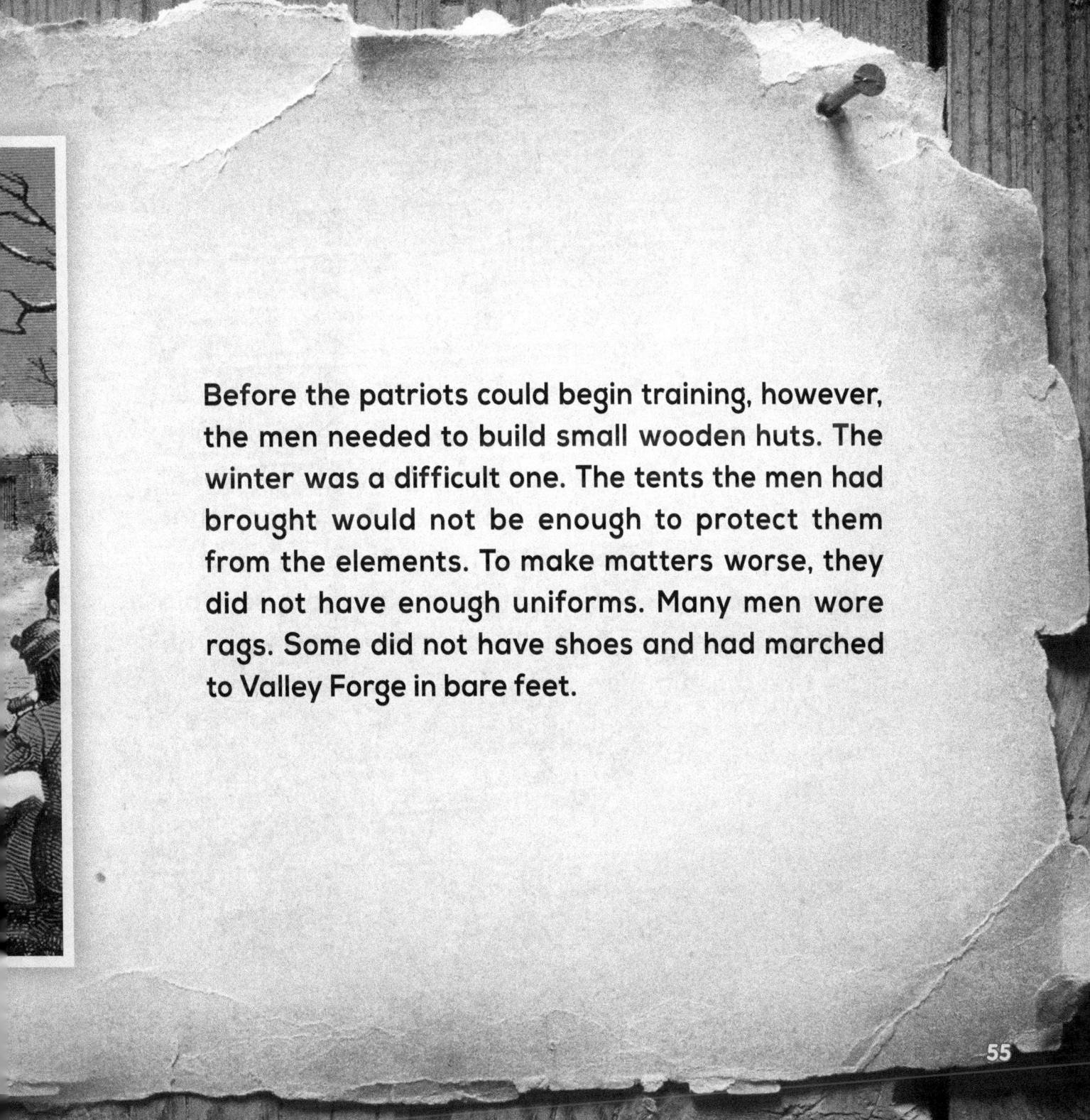

Before the patriots could begin training, however, the men needed to build small wooden huts. The winter was a difficult one. The tents the men had brought would not be enough to protect them from the elements. To make matters worse, they did not have enough uniforms. Many men wore rags. Some did not have shoes and had marched to Valley Forge in bare feet.

Food was also an issue. There was little to be had, and what did arrive was often spoiled. Men would be sent out to hunt and would be so hungry that they would steal from local farmers. Between the cold and malnourishment, disease became a very big problem. Many died from illness; others deserted the army and the numbers dwindled.

Many men died from illness and others deserted the army.

Nevertheless, Washington suffered with his men and was able to inspire their loyalty. He kept the army together. The men who did not desert were trained in proper formation and with proper drills. By the time winter was over, those who had remained made the army stronger than ever.

Washington suffered with his men and inspired their loyalty.

With the support from the French made official with the signing of a treaty between the United States and France, the British opted to leave Philadelphia and reassess their strategy.

American and French representatives signing the Treaty of Alliance in Paris.

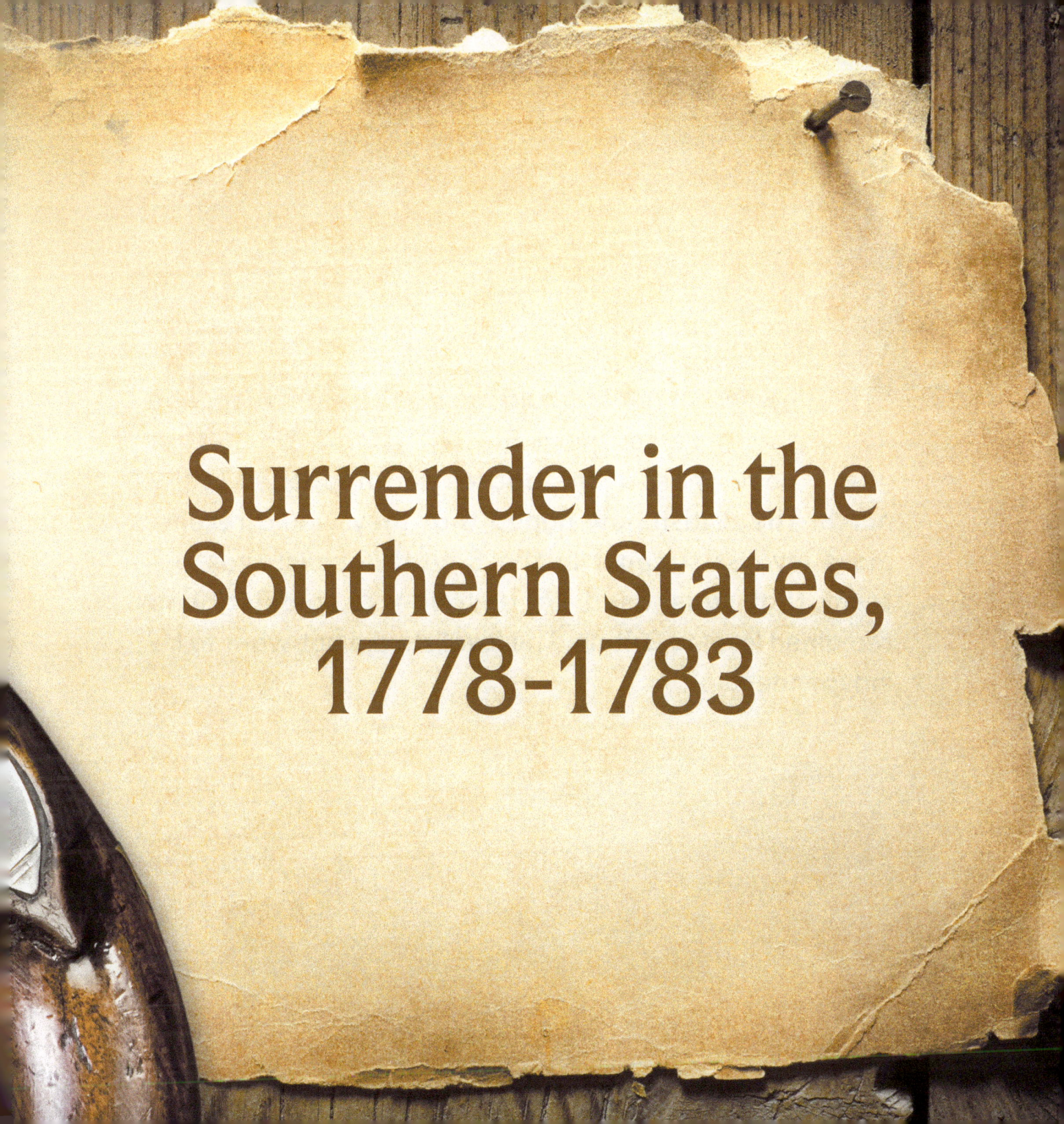

Surrender in the Southern States, 1778-1783

The British felt it would be wise to start attacking the more southern States instead. Up to that point, most of the battles had happened in the north. The British now hoped that they would receive more loyalist support in the South. *Loyalist* was the term that was used to describe a colonist who remained loyal to Britain. The loyalists did not want to be independent.

British troops accompanied by Loyalists.

With their new strategy, the British were able to achieve victory in the cities of Savannah, Georgia and Charleston, South Carolina. These victories were achieved under the British General Cornwallis.

General Charles Cornwallis

Unfortunately for Cornwallis, he would encounter severe resistance from the American troops in Virginia. On October 19, 1781, Cornwallis would surrender in the Battle of Yorktown.

Surrender of British army under commander Cornwallis to Washington and Rochambeau at Yorktown ending the Revolutionary War.

Announcement of the signing of the Treaty of Paris to a crowd gathered at the Tuilleries, 1783.

Although the fighting ceased on the date that Cornwallis surrendered, the war would not end until September of 1783. It took another two years for the American Revolutionary War to end. It would not be officially over until the Treaty of Paris was finally signed.

Many soldiers in the Continental Army struggled with that reality. They wanted to go home and were tired of waiting. They felt frustrated that, as a new country, the United States struggled to pay them on time.

Continental Army disbanding at New Windsor, New York at the end of the Revolutionary War in November of 1783.

A lot of these soldiers banded together and suggested to General George Washington that they take over and make him the new king. However, Washington refused. He did not want to be king after having just fought to be free from being ruled by a king.

George Washington's triumphal entry into New York, 25 November 1783.

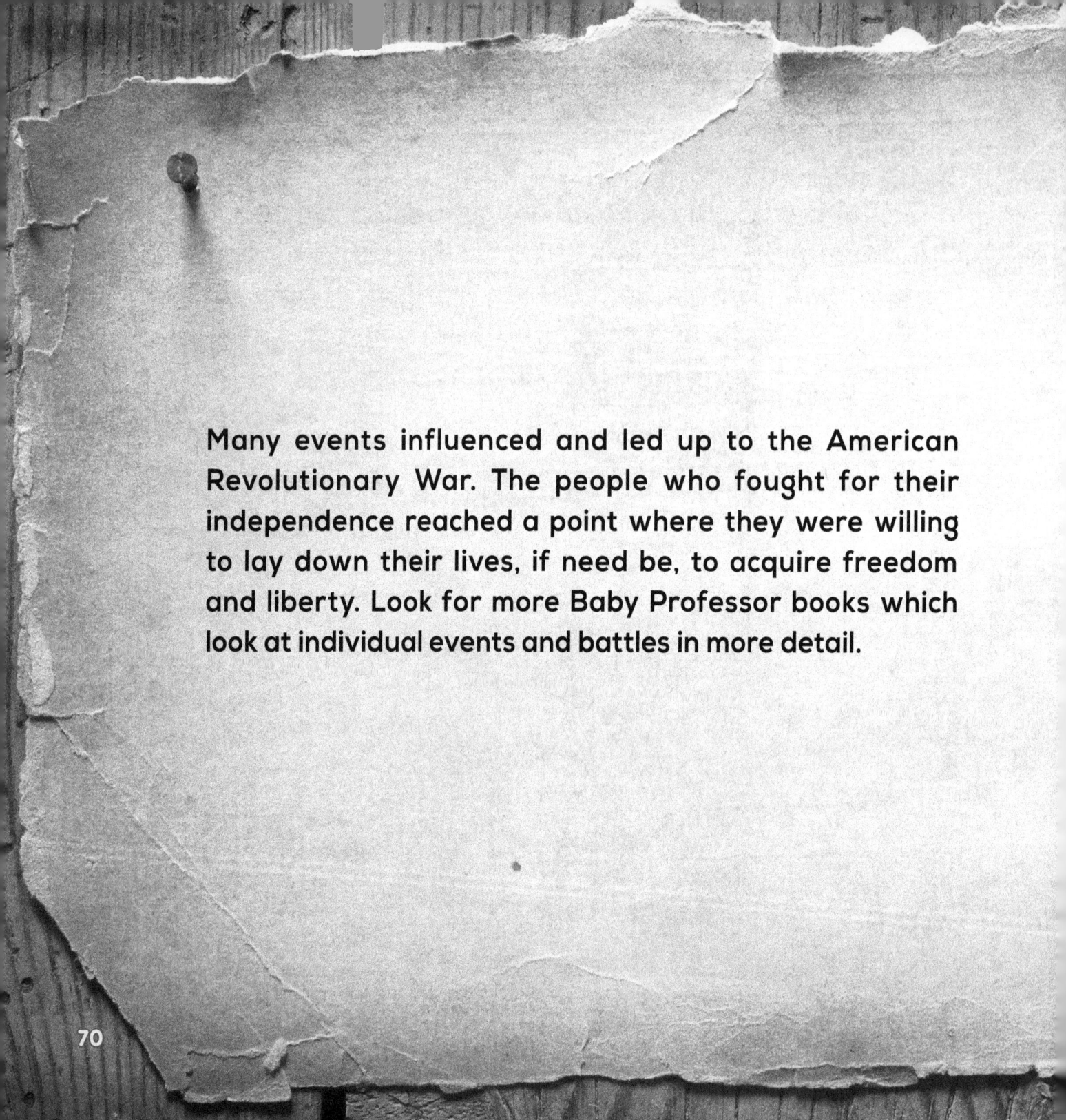

Many events influenced and led up to the American Revolutionary War. The people who fought for their independence reached a point where they were willing to lay down their lives, if need be, to acquire freedom and liberty. Look for more Baby Professor books which look at individual events and battles in more detail.

Visit

www.speedypublishing.com

To view and download free content
on your favorite subject and browse
our catalog of new and exciting
books for readers of all ages.

Lightning Source UK Ltd.
Milton Keynes UK
UKHW051525020121
376250UK00002B/34